2021
SCHOOL DIARY

SCHOOL HOLIDAY DATES 2021

FIRST DAY OF SCHOOL - TERM 1

LAST DAY OF SCHOOL - TERM 1

FIRST DAY OF SCHOOL - TERM 2

LAST DAY OF SCHOOL - TERM 2

FIRST DAY OF SCHOOL - TERM 3

LAST DAY OF SCHOOL - TERM 3

FIRST DAY OF SCHOOL - TERM 4

LAST DAY OF SCHOOL - TERM 4

TERM DATES 2021

TERM 1

TERM 2

TERM 3

TERM 4

OTHER DATES
Eg. School Graduation

SCHOOL CAMPUS MAP

MY 12 MONTH GOALS

Write down the goals you wish to achieve in 2021

PERSONAL GOALS

....
....
....
....
....
....

ACADEMIC GOALS

....
....
....
....
....
....

HEALTH & FITNESS GOALS

....
....
....
....
....
....

What you get by achieving your goals is not as important as what you become by achieving your goals

— Henry David Thoreau —

WEEKLY TIMETABLE   SEMESTER 1

DATE COMMENCING: /   /

DAY	MONDAY	TUESDAY	WEDNESDAY
LESSON 1 *START TIME* :	Subject	Subject	Subject
LESSON 2 *START TIME* :			
LESSON 3 *START TIME* :			
LESSON 4 *START TIME* :			
LESSON 5 *START TIME* :			
LESSON 6 *START TIME* :			
LESSON 7 *START TIME* :			

Other information to note

MY 12 MONTH GOALS

Write down the goals you wish to achieve in 2021

PERSONAL GOALS

....
....
....
....
....
....

ACADEMIC GOALS

....
....
....
....
....
....

HEALTH & FITNESS GOALS

....
....
....
....
....
....

What you get by achieving your goals is not as important as what you become by achieving your goals

—Henry David Thoreau—

WEEKLY TIMETABLE   SEMESTER 1

DATE COMMENCING: /   /

DAY	MONDAY	TUESDAY	WEDNESDAY
LESSON 1 *START TIME :*	Subject	Subject	Subject
LESSON 2 *START TIME :*			
LESSON 3 *START TIME :*			
LESSON 4 *START TIME :*			
LESSON 5 *START TIME :*			
LESSON 6 *START TIME :*			
LESSON 7 *START TIME :*			

Other information to note

THURSDAY	FRIDAY	NOTES
Subject	Subject	

WEEKEND

WEEKLY TIMETABLE   SEMESTER 2

DATE COMMENCING: /   /

DAY	MONDAY	TUESDAY	WEDNESDAY
LESSON 1 *START TIME :*	Subject	Subject	Subject
LESSON 2 *START TIME :*			
LESSON 3 *START TIME :*			
LESSON 4 *START TIME :*			
LESSON 5 *START TIME :*			
LESSON 6 *START TIME :*			
LESSON 7 *START TIME :*			

Other information to note

THURSDAY	FRIDAY	NOTES
Subject	Subject	

WEEKEND

DECEMBER 2020/JANUARY 2021

MONDAY 28

....
....
....
....

┌─ OTHER NOTES/TASKS TO COMPLETE ───┐
│   │
│   │
└──┘

TUESDAY 29

....
....
....
....

┌─ OTHER NOTES/TASKS TO COMPLETE ───┐
│   │
│   │
└──┘

WEDNESDAY 30

....
....
....
....

┌─ OTHER NOTES/TASKS TO COMPLETE ───┐
│   │
│   │
└──┘

THURSDAY 31

....
....
....
....

┌─ OTHER NOTES/TASKS TO COMPLETE ───┐
│   │
│   │
└──┘

FRIDAY 01 - JANUARY 2021

....
....
....
....

SAT 02	**SUN 03**

Homeroom Teacher _____ **Parent Signature** _____

JANUARY 2021

MONDAY 04

....
....
....
....

OTHER NOTES/TASKS TO COMPLETE

TUESDAY 05

....
....
....
....

OTHER NOTES/TASKS TO COMPLETE

WEDNESDAY 06

....
....
....
....

OTHER NOTES/TASKS TO COMPLETE

THURSDAY 07

....
....
....
....

OTHER NOTES/TASKS TO COMPLETE

FRIDAY 08

....
....
....
....

SAT 09	SUN 10

Homeroom Teacher   Parent Signature

JANUARY 2021

MONDAY 11

....
....
....
....

OTHER NOTES/TASKS TO COMPLETE

TUESDAY 12

....
....
....
....

OTHER NOTES/TASKS TO COMPLETE

WEDNESDAY 13

....
....
....
....

OTHER NOTES/TASKS TO COMPLETE

THURSDAY 14

....
....
....
....

OTHER NOTES/TASKS TO COMPLETE

FRIDAY 15

....
....
....
....

SAT 16	SUN 17

Homeroom Teacher _____ Parent Signature _____

My Week Ahead

Start your week by answering the following questions

I am grateful for:

....

....

What will be my act of kindness this week?

....

....

....

I have the following things on this week: Academic exams, sport training, music lessons etc.

....

....

....

....

My Key Focus For This Week:

JANUARY 2021

MONDAY 18

....
....
....
....

OTHER NOTES/TASKS TO COMPLETE

TUESDAY 19

....
....
....
....

OTHER NOTES/TASKS TO COMPLETE

WEDNESDAY 20

....
....
....
....

OTHER NOTES/TASKS TO COMPLETE

THURSDAY 21

....
....
....
....

OTHER NOTES/TASKS TO COMPLETE

FRIDAY 22

....
....
....
....

SAT 23	**SUN 24**

Homeroom Teacher _____   Parent Signature _____

My Week Ahead

Start your week by answering the following questions

I am grateful for:

....

....

What will be my act of kindness this week?

....

....

....

I have the following things on this week: Academic exams, sport training, music lessons etc.

....

....

....

....

....

My Key Focus For This Week:

JANUARY 2021

MONDAY 25

....
....
....
....

┌─ OTHER NOTES/TASKS TO COMPLETE ─────────────────────────┐
│   │
│   │
└──┘

TUESDAY 26

....
....
....
....

┌─ OTHER NOTES/TASKS TO COMPLETE ─────────────────────────┐
│   │
│   │
└──┘

WEDNESDAY 27

....
....
....
....

┌─ OTHER NOTES/TASKS TO COMPLETE ─────────────────────────┐
│   │
│   │
└──┘

THURSDAY 28

....
....
....
....

┌─ OTHER NOTES/TASKS TO COMPLETE ─────────────────────────┐
│   │
│   │
└──┘

FRIDAY 29

....
....
....
....

SAT 30	SUN 31

Homeroom Teacher _____   Parent Signature _____

My Week Ahead

Start your week by answering the following questions

I am grateful for:
....
....

What will be my act of kindness this week?
....
....
....

I have the following things on this week: Academic exams, sport training, music lessons etc.
....
....
....
....
....

My Key Focus For This Week:

FEBRUARY 2021

MONDAY 01

....
....
....
....

┌─ OTHER NOTES/TASKS TO COMPLETE ─────────────────────────────────────┐
│   │
│   │
└──┘

TUESDAY 02

....
....
....
....

┌─ OTHER NOTES/TASKS TO COMPLETE ─────────────────────────────────────┐
│   │
│   │
└──┘

WEDNESDAY 03

....
....
....
....

┌─ OTHER NOTES/TASKS TO COMPLETE ─────────────────────────────────────┐
│   │
│   │
└──┘

THURSDAY 04

....
....
....
....

┌─ OTHER NOTES/TASKS TO COMPLETE ─────────────────────────────────────┐
│   │
│   │
└──┘

FRIDAY 05

....
....
....
....

SAT 06	**SUN 07**

Homeroom Teacher _____   **Parent Signature** _____

My Week Ahead

Start your week by answering the following questions

I am grateful for:

....

....

What will be my act of kindness this week?

....

....

....

I have the following things on this week: Academic exams, sport training, music lessons etc.

....

....

....

....

....

My Key Focus For This Week:

FEBRUARY 2021

MONDAY 08

....
....
....
....

┌─ OTHER NOTES/TASKS TO COMPLETE ───┐
│   │
│   │
└──┘

TUESDAY 09

....
....
....
....

┌─ OTHER NOTES/TASKS TO COMPLETE ───┐
│   │
│   │
└──┘

WEDNESDAY 10

....
....
....
....

┌─ OTHER NOTES/TASKS TO COMPLETE ───┐
│   │
│   │
└──┘

THURSDAY 11

....
....
....
....

┌─ OTHER NOTES/TASKS TO COMPLETE ───┐
│   │
│   │
└──┘

FRIDAY 12

....
....
....
....

SAT 13	**SUN 14**

Homeroom Teacher   **Parent Signature**

My Week Ahead

Start your week by answering the following questions

I am grateful for:

....

....

What will be my act of kindness this week?

....

....

....

I have the following things on this week: *Academic exams, sport training, music lessons etc.*

....

....

....

....

My Key Focus For This Week:

FEBRUARY 2021

MONDAY 15

....
....
....
....

┌─ OTHER NOTES/TASKS TO COMPLETE ──────────────────────────────────┐
│   │
│   │
└──┘

TUESDAY 16

....
....
....
....

┌─ OTHER NOTES/TASKS TO COMPLETE ──────────────────────────────────┐
│   │
│   │
└──┘

WEDNESDAY 17

....
....
....
....

┌─ OTHER NOTES/TASKS TO COMPLETE ──────────────────────────────────┐
│   │
│   │
└──┘

THURSDAY 18

....
....
....
....

┌─ OTHER NOTES/TASKS TO COMPLETE ──────────────────────────────────┐
│   │
│   │
└──┘

FRIDAY 19

....
....
....
....

SAT 20	SUN 21

Homeroom Teacher _____   **Parent Signature** _____

My Week Ahead

Start your week by answering the following questions

I am grateful for:

....

....

What will be my act of kindness this week?

....

....

....

I have the following things on this week: Academic exams, sport training, music lessons etc.

....

....

....

....

My Key Focus For This Week:

FEBRUARY 2021

MONDAY 22

....
....
....
....

┌─ OTHER NOTES/TASKS TO COMPLETE ───┐
│   │
│   │
└──┘

TUESDAY 23

....
....
....
....

┌─ OTHER NOTES/TASKS TO COMPLETE ───┐
│   │
│   │
└──┘

WEDNESDAY 24

....
....
....
....

┌─ OTHER NOTES/TASKS TO COMPLETE ───┐
│   │
│   │
└──┘

THURSDAY 25

....
....
....
....

┌─ OTHER NOTES/TASKS TO COMPLETE ───┐
│   │
│   │
└──┘

FRIDAY 26

....
....
....
....

SAT 27	SUN 28

Homeroom Teacher _____   Parent Signature _____

My Week Ahead

Start your week by answering the following questions

I am grateful for:

....

....

What will be my act of kindness this week?

....

....

....

I have the following things on this week: Academic exams, sport training, music lessons etc.

....

....

....

....

My Key Focus For This Week:

MARCH 2021

MONDAY 01

....
....
....
....

┌─ OTHER NOTES/TASKS TO COMPLETE ─────────────────────┐
│   │
│   │
└──┘

TUESDAY 02

....
....
....
....

┌─ OTHER NOTES/TASKS TO COMPLETE ─────────────────────┐
│   │
│   │
└──┘

WEDNESDAY 03

....
....
....
....

┌─ OTHER NOTES/TASKS TO COMPLETE ─────────────────────┐
│   │
│   │
└──┘

THURSDAY 04

....
....
....
....

┌─ OTHER NOTES/TASKS TO COMPLETE ─────────────────────┐
│   │
│   │
└──┘

FRIDAY 05

....
....
....
....

SAT 06	SUN 07

Homeroom Teacher _____   Parent Signature _____

My Week Ahead

Start your week by answering the following questions

I am grateful for:

....
....

What will be my act of kindness this week?

....
....
....

I have the following things on this week: Academic exams, sport training, music lessons etc.

....
....
....
....
....

My Key Focus For This Week:

MARCH 2021

MONDAY 08

....
....
....
....

┌─ OTHER NOTES/TASKS TO COMPLETE ─────────────────────────────────┐
│   │
│   │
└───┘

TUESDAY 09

....
....
....
....

┌─ OTHER NOTES/TASKS TO COMPLETE ─────────────────────────────────┐
│   │
│   │
└───┘

WEDNESDAY 10

....
....
....
....

┌─ OTHER NOTES/TASKS TO COMPLETE ─────────────────────────────────┐
│   │
│   │
└───┘

THURSDAY 11

....
....
....
....

┌─ OTHER NOTES/TASKS TO COMPLETE ─────────────────────────────────┐
│   │
│   │
└───┘

FRIDAY 12

....
....
....
....

SAT 13	SUN 14

Homeroom Teacher _____   Parent Signature _____

My Week Ahead

Start your week by answering the following questions

I am grateful for:

....

....

What will be my act of kindness this week?

....

....

....

I have the following things on this week: Academic exams, sport training, music lessons etc.

....

....

....

....

My Key Focus For This Week:

MARCH 2021

MONDAY 15

....
....
....
....

┌─ OTHER NOTES/TASKS TO COMPLETE ─────────────────────────────────────┐
│   │
│   │
└──┘

TUESDAY 16

....
....
....
....

┌─ OTHER NOTES/TASKS TO COMPLETE ─────────────────────────────────────┐
│   │
│   │
└──┘

WEDNESDAY 17

....
....
....
....

┌─ OTHER NOTES/TASKS TO COMPLETE ─────────────────────────────────────┐
│   │
│   │
└──┘

THURSDAY 18

....
....
....
....

┌─ OTHER NOTES/TASKS TO COMPLETE ─────────────────────────────────────┐
│   │
│   │
└──┘

FRIDAY 19

....
....
....
....

SAT 20	SUN 21

Homeroom Teacher_____   **Parent Signature**_____

My Week Ahead

Start your week by answering the following questions

I am grateful for:

....

....

What will be my act of kindness this week?

....

....

....

I have the following things on this week: Academic exams, sport training, music lessons etc.

....

....

....

....

....

My Key Focus For This Week:

MARCH 2021

MONDAY 22

....
....
....
....

┌─ OTHER NOTES/TASKS TO COMPLETE ─────────────────────────────────┐
│   │
│   │
└───┘

TUESDAY 23

....
....
....
....

┌─ OTHER NOTES/TASKS TO COMPLETE ─────────────────────────────────┐
│   │
│   │
└───┘

WEDNESDAY 24

....
....
....
....

┌─ OTHER NOTES/TASKS TO COMPLETE ─────────────────────────────────┐
│   │
│   │
└───┘

THURSDAY 25

....
....
....
....

┌─ OTHER NOTES/TASKS TO COMPLETE ─────────────────────────────────┐
│   │
│   │
└───┘

FRIDAY 26

....
....
....
....

SAT 27	SUN 28

Homeroom Teacher _____   **Parent Signature** _____

My Week Ahead

Start your week by answering the following questions

I am grateful for:

....

....

What will be my act of kindness this week?

....

....

....

I have the following things on this week: *Academic exams, sport training, music lessons etc.*

....

....

....

....

My Key Focus For This Week:

MARCH/APRIL 2021

MONDAY 29

....
....
....
....

OTHER NOTES/TASKS TO COMPLETE

TUESDAY 30

....
....
....
....

OTHER NOTES/TASKS TO COMPLETE

WEDNESDAY 31

....
....
....
....

OTHER NOTES/TASKS TO COMPLETE

THURSDAY 01 APRIL

....
....
....
....

OTHER NOTES/TASKS TO COMPLETE

FRIDAY 02

....
....
....
....

SAT 03	SUN 04

Homeroom Teacher _____ Parent Signature _____

My Week Ahead

Start your week by answering the following questions

I am grateful for:

....

....

What will be my act of kindness this week?

....

....

I have the following things on this week: Academic exams, sport training, music lessons etc.

....

....

....

....

....

My Key Focus For This Week:

APRIL 2021

MONDAY 05

....
....
....
....

┌─ OTHER NOTES/TASKS TO COMPLETE ───┐
│   │
│   │
└──┘

TUESDAY 06

....
....
....
....

┌─ OTHER NOTES/TASKS TO COMPLETE ───┐
│   │
│   │
└──┘

WEDNESDAY 07

....
....
....
....

┌─ OTHER NOTES/TASKS TO COMPLETE ───┐
│   │
│   │
└──┘

THURSDAY 08

....
....
....
....

┌─ OTHER NOTES/TASKS TO COMPLETE ───┐
│   │
│   │
└──┘

FRIDAY 09

....
....
....
....

SAT 10	SUN 11

Homeroom Teacher _____   Parent Signature _____

My Week Ahead

Start your week by answering the following questions

I am grateful for:

....
....

What will be my act of kindness this week?

....
....
....

I have the following things on this week: *Academic exams, sport training, music lessons etc.*

....
....
....
....

My Key Focus For This Week:

APRIL 2021

MONDAY 12

....
....
....
....

┌─ OTHER NOTES/TASKS TO COMPLETE ─────────────────────────────────┐
│   │
│   │
└───┘

TUESDAY 13

....
....
....
....

┌─ OTHER NOTES/TASKS TO COMPLETE ─────────────────────────────────┐
│   │
│   │
└───┘

WEDNESDAY 14

....
....
....
....

┌─ OTHER NOTES/TASKS TO COMPLETE ─────────────────────────────────┐
│   │
│   │
└───┘

THURSDAY 15

....
....
....
....

┌─ OTHER NOTES/TASKS TO COMPLETE ─────────────────────────────────┐
│   │
│   │
└───┘

FRIDAY 16

....
....
....
....

SAT 17	SUN 18

Homeroom Teacher _____   Parent Signature _____

My Week Ahead

Start your week by answering the following questions

I am grateful for:

....

....

What will be my act of kindness this week?

....

....

....

I have the following things on this week: Academic exams, sport training, music lessons etc.

....

....

....

....

....

My Key Focus For This Week:

APRIL 2021

MONDAY 19

....
....
....
....

┌─ OTHER NOTES/TASKS TO COMPLETE ─────────────────────┐
│   │
│   │
└───┘

TUESDAY 20

....
....
....
....

┌─ OTHER NOTES/TASKS TO COMPLETE ─────────────────────┐
│   │
│   │
└───┘

WEDNESDAY 21

....
....
....
....

┌─ OTHER NOTES/TASKS TO COMPLETE ─────────────────────┐
│   │
│   │
└───┘

THURSDAY 22

....
....
....
....

┌─ OTHER NOTES/TASKS TO COMPLETE ─────────────────────┐
│   │
│   │
└───┘

FRIDAY 23

....
....
....
....

SAT 24	**SUN 25**

Homeroom Teacher _____   **Parent Signature** _____

My Week Ahead

Start your week by answering the following questions

I am grateful for:

....

....

What will be my act of kindness this week?

....

....

I have the following things on this week: *Academic exams, sport training, music lessons etc.*

....

....

....

....

My Key Focus For This Week:

APRIL/MAY 2021

MONDAY 26

....
....
....
....

OTHER NOTES/TASKS TO COMPLETE

TUESDAY 27

....
....
....
....

OTHER NOTES/TASKS TO COMPLETE

WEDNESDAY 28

....
....
....
....

OTHER NOTES/TASKS TO COMPLETE

THURSDAY 29

....
....
....
....

OTHER NOTES/TASKS TO COMPLETE

FRIDAY 30

....
....
....
....

SAT 01	SUN 02

Homeroom Teacher _____   Parent Signature _____

My Week Ahead

Start your week by answering the following questions

I am grateful for:

....

....

What will be my act of kindness this week?

....

....

....

I have the following things on this week: Academic exams, sport training, music lessons etc.

....

....

....

....

....

My Key Focus For This Week:

MAY 2021

MONDAY 03

....
....
....
....

┌─ OTHER NOTES/TASKS TO COMPLETE ─────────────────────────────────────┐
│   │
│   │
└──┘

TUESDAY 04

....
....
....
....

┌─ OTHER NOTES/TASKS TO COMPLETE ─────────────────────────────────────┐
│   │
│   │
└──┘

WEDNESDAY 05

....
....
....
....

┌─ OTHER NOTES/TASKS TO COMPLETE ─────────────────────────────────────┐
│   │
│   │
└──┘

THURSDAY 06

....
....
....
....

┌─ OTHER NOTES/TASKS TO COMPLETE ─────────────────────────────────────┐
│   │
│   │
└──┘

FRIDAY 07

....
....
....
....

SAT 08	**SUN 09**

Homeroom Teacher _____   **Parent Signature** _____

My Week Ahead

Start your week by answering the following questions

I am grateful for:

....

....

What will be my act of kindness this week?

....

....

....

I have the following things on this week: *Academic exams, sport training, music lessons etc.*

....

....

....

....

My Key Focus For This Week:

MAY 2021

MONDAY 10

....
....
....
....

- OTHER NOTES/TASKS TO COMPLETE

TUESDAY 11

....
....
....
....

- OTHER NOTES/TASKS TO COMPLETE

WEDNESDAY 12

....
....
....
....

- OTHER NOTES/TASKS TO COMPLETE

THURSDAY 13

....
....
....
....

- OTHER NOTES/TASKS TO COMPLETE

FRIDAY 14

....
....
....
....

SAT 15	SUN 16

Homeroom Teacher_____ **Parent Signature**_____

My Week Ahead

Start your week by answering the following questions

I am grateful for:

....

....

What will be my act of kindness this week?

....

....

....

I have the following things on this week: *Academic exams, sport training, music lessons etc.*

....

....

....

....

My Key Focus For This Week:

MAY 2021

MONDAY 17

....
....
....
....

┌─ OTHER NOTES/TASKS TO COMPLETE ────────────────────────┐
│   │
│   │
└───┘

TUESDAY 18

....
....
....
....

┌─ OTHER NOTES/TASKS TO COMPLETE ────────────────────────┐
│   │
│   │
└───┘

WEDNESDAY 19

....
....
....
....

┌─ OTHER NOTES/TASKS TO COMPLETE ────────────────────────┐
│   │
│   │
└───┘

THURSDAY 20

....
....
....
....

┌─ OTHER NOTES/TASKS TO COMPLETE ────────────────────────┐
│   │
│   │
└───┘

FRIDAY 21

....
....
....
....

SAT 22	**SUN 23**

Homeroom Teacher_____   **Parent Signature**_____

My Week Ahead

Start your week by answering the following questions

I am grateful for:

....

....

What will be my act of kindness this week?

....

....

....

I have the following things on this week: *Academic exams, sport training, music lessons etc.*

....

....

....

....

My Key Focus For This Week:

MAY 2021

MONDAY 24

....
....
....
....

┌─ OTHER NOTES/TASKS TO COMPLETE ──────────────────────────────────────┐
│   │
│   │
└──┘

TUESDAY 25

....
....
....
....

┌─ OTHER NOTES/TASKS TO COMPLETE ──────────────────────────────────────┐
│   │
│   │
└──┘

WEDNESDAY 26

....
....
....
....

┌─ OTHER NOTES/TASKS TO COMPLETE ──────────────────────────────────────┐
│   │
│   │
└──┘

THURSDAY 27

....
....
....
....

┌─ OTHER NOTES/TASKS TO COMPLETE ──────────────────────────────────────┐
│   │
│   │
└──┘

FRIDAY 28

....
....
....
....

SAT 29	**SUN 30**

Homeroom Teacher _____ **Parent Signature** _____

My Week Ahead

Start your week by answering the following questions

I am grateful for:

....

....

What will be my act of kindness this week?

....

....

....

I have the following things on this week: Academic exams, sport training, music lessons etc.

....

....

....

....

My Key Focus For This Week:

MAY/JUNE 2021

MONDAY 31

....
....
....
....

┌─ OTHER NOTES/TASKS TO COMPLETE ─────────────────────────────────┐
│   │
│   │
└──┘

TUESDAY 01

....
....
....
....

┌─ OTHER NOTES/TASKS TO COMPLETE ─────────────────────────────────┐
│   │
│   │
└──┘

WEDNESDAY 02

....
....
....
....

┌─ OTHER NOTES/TASKS TO COMPLETE ─────────────────────────────────┐
│   │
│   │
└──┘

THURSDAY 03

....
....
....
....

┌─ OTHER NOTES/TASKS TO COMPLETE ─────────────────────────────────┐
│   │
│   │
└──┘

FRIDAY 04

....
....
....
....

SAT 05	**SUN 06**

Homeroom Teacher _____ **Parent Signature** _____

My Week Ahead

Start your week by answering the following questions

I am grateful for:

....

....

What will be my act of kindness this week?

....

....

....

I have the following things on this week: Academic exams, sport training, music lessons etc.

....

....

....

....

My Key Focus For This Week:

JUNE 2021

MONDAY 07

OTHER NOTES/TASKS TO COMPLETE

TUESDAY 08

OTHER NOTES/TASKS TO COMPLETE

WEDNESDAY 09

OTHER NOTES/TASKS TO COMPLETE

THURSDAY 10

OTHER NOTES/TASKS TO COMPLETE

FRIDAY 11

SAT 12	SUN 13

Homeroom Teacher_____   Parent Signature_____

My Week Ahead

Start your week by answering the following questions

I am grateful for:
....
....

What will be my act of kindness this week?
....
....
....

I have the following things on this week: *Academic exams, sport training, music lessons etc.*
....
....
....
....

My Key Focus For This Week:

JUNE 2021

MONDAY 14

....
....
....
....

┌─ OTHER NOTES/TASKS TO COMPLETE ─────────────────────────────┐
│   │
│   │
└──┘

TUESDAY 15

....
....
....
....

┌─ OTHER NOTES/TASKS TO COMPLETE ─────────────────────────────┐
│   │
│   │
└──┘

WEDNESDAY 16

....
....
....
....

┌─ OTHER NOTES/TASKS TO COMPLETE ─────────────────────────────┐
│   │
│   │
└──┘

THURSDAY 17

....
....
....
....

┌─ OTHER NOTES/TASKS TO COMPLETE ─────────────────────────────┐
│   │
│   │
└──┘

FRIDAY 18

....
....
....
....

SAT 19	SUN 20

Homeroom Teacher _____   Parent Signature _____

My Week Ahead

Start your week by answering the following questions

I am grateful for:
....
....

What will be my act of kindness this week?
....
....

I have the following things on this week: *Academic exams, sport training, music lessons etc.*
....
....
....
....

My Key Focus For This Week:

JUNE 2021

MONDAY 21

....
....
....
....

┌─ OTHER NOTES/TASKS TO COMPLETE ─────────────────────────────┐
│   │
│   │
└──┘

TUESDAY 22

....
....
....
....

┌─ OTHER NOTES/TASKS TO COMPLETE ─────────────────────────────┐
│   │
│   │
└──┘

WEDNESDAY 23

....
....
....
....

┌─ OTHER NOTES/TASKS TO COMPLETE ─────────────────────────────┐
│   │
│   │
└──┘

THURSDAY 24

....
....
....
....

┌─ OTHER NOTES/TASKS TO COMPLETE ─────────────────────────────┐
│   │
│   │
└──┘

FRIDAY 25

....
....
....
....

SAT 26	**SUN 27**

Homeroom Teacher _____   **Parent Signature** _____

My Week Ahead

Start your week by answering the following questions

I am grateful for:

....
....

What will be my act of kindness this week?

....
....
....

I have the following things on this week: Academic exams, sport training, music lessons etc.

....
....
....
....
....

My Key Focus For This Week:

JUNE/JULY 2021

MONDAY 28

....
....
....
....

OTHER NOTES/TASKS TO COMPLETE

TUESDAY 29

....
....
....
....

OTHER NOTES/TASKS TO COMPLETE

WEDNESDAY 30

....
....
....
....

OTHER NOTES/TASKS TO COMPLETE

THURSDAY 1st July

....
....
....
....

OTHER NOTES/TASKS TO COMPLETE

FRIDAY 02

....
....
....
....

SAT 03	SUN 04

Homeroom Teacher _____   Parent Signature _____

My Week Ahead

Start your week by answering the following questions

I am grateful for:

....

....

What will be my act of kindness this week?

....

....

....

I have the following things on this week: Academic exams, sport training, music lessons etc.

....

....

....

....

My Key Focus For This Week:

JULY 2021

MONDAY 05

....
....
....
....

┌─ OTHER NOTES/TASKS TO COMPLETE ─────────────────────────────────────┐
│   │
└──┘

TUESDAY 06

....
....
....
....

┌─ OTHER NOTES/TASKS TO COMPLETE ─────────────────────────────────────┐
│   │
└──┘

WEDNESDAY 07

....
....
....
....

┌─ OTHER NOTES/TASKS TO COMPLETE ─────────────────────────────────────┐
│   │
└──┘

THURSDAY 08

....
....
....
....

┌─ OTHER NOTES/TASKS TO COMPLETE ─────────────────────────────────────┐
│   │
└──┘

FRIDAY 09

....
....
....
....

SAT 10	**SUN 11**

Homeroom Teacher_____   **Parent Signature**_____

My Week Ahead

Start your week by answering the following questions

I am grateful for:

....

....

What will be my act of kindness this week?

....

....

....

I have the following things on this week: Academic exams, sport training, music lessons etc.

....

....

....

....

My Key Focus For This Week:

JULY 2021

MONDAY 12

....
....
....
....

┌─ OTHER NOTES/TASKS TO COMPLETE ─────────────────────────┐
│   │
│   │
└──┘

TUESDAY 13

....
....
....
....

┌─ OTHER NOTES/TASKS TO COMPLETE ─────────────────────────┐
│   │
│   │
└──┘

WEDNESDAY 14

....
....
....
....

┌─ OTHER NOTES/TASKS TO COMPLETE ─────────────────────────┐
│   │
│   │
└──┘

THURSDAY 15

....
....
....
....

┌─ OTHER NOTES/TASKS TO COMPLETE ─────────────────────────┐
│   │
│   │
└──┘

FRIDAY 16

....
....
....
....

SAT 17	SUN 18

Homeroom Teacher _____   Parent Signature _____

My Week Ahead

Start your week by answering the following questions

I am grateful for:

....

....

What will be my act of kindness this week?

....

....

....

I have the following things on this week: *Academic exams, sport training, music lessons etc.*

....

....

....

....

My Key Focus For This Week:

JULY 2021

MONDAY 19

....
....
....
....

┌─ OTHER NOTES/TASKS TO COMPLETE ───┐
│   │
│   │
└──┘

TUESDAY 20

....
....
....
....

┌─ OTHER NOTES/TASKS TO COMPLETE ───┐
│   │
│   │
└──┘

WEDNESDAY 21

....
....
....
....

┌─ OTHER NOTES/TASKS TO COMPLETE ───┐
│   │
│   │
└──┘

THURSDAY 22

....
....
....
....

┌─ OTHER NOTES/TASKS TO COMPLETE ───┐
│   │
│   │
└──┘

FRIDAY 23

....
....
....
....

SAT 24	**SUN 25**

Homeroom Teacher _____   Parent Signature _____

My Week Ahead

Start your week by answering the following questions

I am grateful for:

....

....

What will be my act of kindness this week?

....

....

....

I have the following things on this week: Academic exams, sport training, music lessons etc.

....

....

....

....

....

My Key Focus For This Week:

JULY/AUGUST 2021

MONDAY 26

....
....
....
....

┌─ OTHER NOTES/TASKS TO COMPLETE ─────────────────────────┐
│   │
│   │
└──┘

TUESDAY 27

....
....
....
....

┌─ OTHER NOTES/TASKS TO COMPLETE ─────────────────────────┐
│   │
│   │
└──┘

WEDNESDAY 28

....
....
....
....

┌─ OTHER NOTES/TASKS TO COMPLETE ─────────────────────────┐
│   │
│   │
└──┘

THURSDAY 29

....
....
....
....

┌─ OTHER NOTES/TASKS TO COMPLETE ─────────────────────────┐
│   │
│   │
└──┘

FRIDAY 30

....
....
....
....

SAT 31	SUN 01

Homeroom Teacher _____ **Parent Signature** _____

My Week Ahead

Start your week by answering the following questions

I am grateful for:

....

....

What will be my act of kindness this week?

....

....

....

I have the following things on this week: Academic exams, sport training, music lessons etc.

....

....

....

....

My Key Focus For This Week:

AUGUST 2021

MONDAY 02

....
....
....
....

┌─ OTHER NOTES/TASKS TO COMPLETE ──────────────────────────────────┐
│   │
│   │
└──┘

TUESDAY 03

....
....
....
....

┌─ OTHER NOTES/TASKS TO COMPLETE ──────────────────────────────────┐
│   │
│   │
└──┘

WEDNESDAY 04

....
....
....
....

┌─ OTHER NOTES/TASKS TO COMPLETE ──────────────────────────────────┐
│   │
│   │
└──┘

THURSDAY 05

....
....
....
....

┌─ OTHER NOTES/TASKS TO COMPLETE ──────────────────────────────────┐
│   │
│   │
└──┘

FRIDAY 06

....
....
....
....

SAT 07	SUN 08

Homeroom Teacher _____   **Parent Signature** _____

My Week Ahead

Start your week by answering the following questions

I am grateful for:
....
....

What will be my act of kindness this week?
....
....
....

I have the following things on this week: Academic exams, sport training, music lessons etc.
....
....
....
....
....

My Key Focus For This Week:

AUGUST 2021

MONDAY 09

....
....
....
....

┌─ OTHER NOTES/TASKS TO COMPLETE ─────────────────────────────────┐
│   │
│   │
└───┘

TUESDAY 10

....
....
....
....

┌─ OTHER NOTES/TASKS TO COMPLETE ─────────────────────────────────┐
│   │
│   │
└───┘

WEDNESDAY 11

....
....
....
....

┌─ OTHER NOTES/TASKS TO COMPLETE ─────────────────────────────────┐
│   │
│   │
└───┘

THURSDAY 12

....
....
....
....

┌─ OTHER NOTES/TASKS TO COMPLETE ─────────────────────────────────┐
│   │
│   │
└───┘

FRIDAY 13

....
....
....
....

SAT 14	SUN 15

Homeroom Teacher _____   **Parent Signature** _____

My Week Ahead

Start your week by answering the following questions

I am grateful for:

....

....

What will be my act of kindness this week?

....

....

....

I have the following things on this week: Academic exams, sport training, music lessons etc.

....

....

....

....

My Key Focus For This Week:

AUGUST 2021

MONDAY 16

....
....
....
....

┌─ OTHER NOTES/TASKS TO COMPLETE ─────────────────┐
│   │
│   │
└───┘

TUESDAY 17

....
....
....
....

┌─ OTHER NOTES/TASKS TO COMPLETE ─────────────────┐
│   │
│   │
└───┘

WEDNESDAY 18

....
....
....
....

┌─ OTHER NOTES/TASKS TO COMPLETE ─────────────────┐
│   │
│   │
└───┘

THURSDAY 19

....
....
....
....

┌─ OTHER NOTES/TASKS TO COMPLETE ─────────────────┐
│   │
│   │
└───┘

FRIDAY 20

....
....
....
....

SAT 21	SUN 22

Homeroom Teacher _____ **Parent Signature** _____

My Week Ahead

Start your week by answering the following questions

I am grateful for:

....

....

What will be my act of kindness this week?

....

....

....

I have the following things on this week: Academic exams, sport training, music lessons etc.

....

....

....

....

My Key Focus For This Week:

AUGUST 2021

MONDAY 23

OTHER NOTES/TASKS TO COMPLETE

TUESDAY 24

OTHER NOTES/TASKS TO COMPLETE

WEDNESDAY 25

OTHER NOTES/TASKS TO COMPLETE

THURSDAY 26

OTHER NOTES/TASKS TO COMPLETE

FRIDAY 27

SAT 28	SUN 29

Homeroom Teacher_____   Parent Signature_____

My Week Ahead

Start your week by answering the following questions

I am grateful for:

....

....

What will be my act of kindness this week?

....

....

....

I have the following things on this week: Academic exams, sport training, music lessons etc.

....

....

....

....

My Key Focus For This Week:

AUGUST/SEPTEMBER 2021

MONDAY 30

....
....
....
....

┌─ OTHER NOTES/TASKS TO COMPLETE ───┐
│   │
└──┘

TUESDAY 31

....
....
....
....

┌─ OTHER NOTES/TASKS TO COMPLETE ───┐
│   │
└──┘

WEDNESDAY 01

....
....
....
....

┌─ OTHER NOTES/TASKS TO COMPLETE ───┐
│   │
└──┘

THURSDAY 02

....
....
....
....

┌─ OTHER NOTES/TASKS TO COMPLETE ───┐
│   │
└──┘

FRIDAY 03

....
....
....
....

SAT 04	SUN 05

Homeroom Teacher _____   **Parent Signature** _____

My Week Ahead

Start your week by answering the following questions

I am grateful for:

....
....

What will be my act of kindness this week?

....
....
....

I have the following things on this week: Academic exams, sport training, music lessons etc.

....
....
....
....
....

My Key Focus For This Week:

SEPTEMBER 2021

MONDAY 06

....
....
....
....

┌─ OTHER NOTES/TASKS TO COMPLETE ───┐
│   │
│   │
└──┘

TUESDAY 07

....
....
....
....

┌─ OTHER NOTES/TASKS TO COMPLETE ───┐
│   │
│   │
└──┘

WEDNESDAY 08

....
....
....
....

┌─ OTHER NOTES/TASKS TO COMPLETE ───┐
│   │
│   │
└──┘

THURSDAY 09

....
....
....
....

┌─ OTHER NOTES/TASKS TO COMPLETE ───┐
│   │
│   │
└──┘

FRIDAY 10

....
....
....
....

SAT 11	SUN 12

Homeroom Teacher _____   Parent Signature _____

My Week Ahead

Start your week by answering the following questions

I am grateful for:

....

....

What will be my act of kindness this week?

....

....

....

I have the following things on this week: Academic exams, sport training, music lessons etc.

....

....

....

....

My Key Focus For This Week:

SEPTEMBER 2021

MONDAY 13

....
....
....
....

┌─ OTHER NOTES/TASKS TO COMPLETE ─────────────────────────────┐
│   │
│   │
└──┘

TUESDAY 14

....
....
....
....

┌─ OTHER NOTES/TASKS TO COMPLETE ─────────────────────────────┐
│   │
│   │
└──┘

WEDNESDAY 15

....
....
....
....

┌─ OTHER NOTES/TASKS TO COMPLETE ─────────────────────────────┐
│   │
│   │
└──┘

THURSDAY 16

....
....
....
....

┌─ OTHER NOTES/TASKS TO COMPLETE ─────────────────────────────┐
│   │
│   │
└──┘

FRIDAY 17

....
....
....
....

SAT 18	SUN 19

Homeroom Teacher_____   Parent Signature_____

My Week Ahead

Start your week by answering the following questions

I am grateful for:

....

....

What will be my act of kindness this week?

....

....

....

I have the following things on this week: Academic exams, sport training, music lessons etc.

....

....

....

....

....

My Key Focus For This Week:

SEPTEMBER 2021

MONDAY 20

....
....
....
....

┌─ OTHER NOTES/TASKS TO COMPLETE ─────────────────────────────┐
│   │
│   │
└──┘

TUESDAY 21

....
....
....
....

┌─ OTHER NOTES/TASKS TO COMPLETE ─────────────────────────────┐
│   │
│   │
└──┘

WEDNESDAY 22

....
....
....
....

┌─ OTHER NOTES/TASKS TO COMPLETE ─────────────────────────────┐
│   │
│   │
└──┘

THURSDAY 23

....
....
....
....

┌─ OTHER NOTES/TASKS TO COMPLETE ─────────────────────────────┐
│   │
│   │
└──┘

FRIDAY 24

....
....
....
....

SAT 25	SUN 26

Homeroom Teacher _____ **Parent Signature** _____

My Week Ahead

Start your week by answering the following questions

I am grateful for:

....

....

What will be my act of kindness this week?

....

....

....

I have the following things on this week: Academic exams, sport training, music lessons etc.

....

....

....

....

....

My Key Focus For This Week:

SEPTEMBER/OCTOBER 2021

MONDAY 27

....
....
....
....

┌─ OTHER NOTES/TASKS TO COMPLETE ────────────────────────────────┐
│   │
│   │
└──┘

TUESDAY 28

....
....
....
....

┌─ OTHER NOTES/TASKS TO COMPLETE ────────────────────────────────┐
│   │
│   │
└──┘

WEDNESDAY 29

....
....
....
....

┌─ OTHER NOTES/TASKS TO COMPLETE ────────────────────────────────┐
│   │
│   │
└──┘

THURSDAY 30

....
....
....
....

┌─ OTHER NOTES/TASKS TO COMPLETE ────────────────────────────────┐
│   │
│   │
└──┘

FRIDAY 01 OCTOBER

....
....
....
....

SAT 02	SUN 03

Homeroom Teacher _____   **Parent Signature** _____

My Week Ahead

Start your week by answering the following questions

I am grateful for:

....
....

What will be my act of kindness this week?

....
....
....

I have the following things on this week: Academic exams, sport training, music lessons etc.

....
....
....
....
....

My Key Focus For This Week:

OCTOBER 2021

MONDAY 04

....
....
....
....

┌─ OTHER NOTES/TASKS TO COMPLETE ───┐
│   │
│   │
└──┘

TUESDAY 05

....
....
....
....

┌─ OTHER NOTES/TASKS TO COMPLETE ───┐
│   │
│   │
└──┘

WEDNESDAY 06

....
....
....
....

┌─ OTHER NOTES/TASKS TO COMPLETE ───┐
│   │
│   │
└──┘

THURSDAY 07

....
....
....
....

┌─ OTHER NOTES/TASKS TO COMPLETE ───┐
│   │
│   │
└──┘

FRIDAY 08

....
....
....
....

SAT 09	SUN 10

Homeroom Teacher _____   Parent Signature _____

My Week Ahead

Start your week by answering the following questions

I am grateful for:

....

....

What will be my act of kindness this week?

....

....

....

I have the following things on this week: Academic exams, sport training, music lessons etc.

....

....

....

....

My Key Focus For This Week:

OCTOBER 2021

MONDAY 11

....
....
....
....

```
┌─ OTHER NOTES/TASKS TO COMPLETE ──────────────────────────────┐
│                                                              │
│                                                              │
└──────────────────────────────────────────────────────────────┘
```

TUESDAY 12

....
....
....
....

```
┌─ OTHER NOTES/TASKS TO COMPLETE ──────────────────────────────┐
│                                                              │
│                                                              │
└──────────────────────────────────────────────────────────────┘
```

WEDNESDAY 13

....
....
....
....

```
┌─ OTHER NOTES/TASKS TO COMPLETE ──────────────────────────────┐
│                                                              │
│                                                              │
└──────────────────────────────────────────────────────────────┘
```

THURSDAY 14

....
....
....
....

```
┌─ OTHER NOTES/TASKS TO COMPLETE ──────────────────────────────┐
│                                                              │
│                                                              │
└──────────────────────────────────────────────────────────────┘
```

FRIDAY 15

....
....
....
....

SAT 16	SUN 17

Homeroom Teacher _____ **Parent Signature** _____

My Week Ahead

Start your week by answering the following questions

I am grateful for:

....

....

What will be my act of kindness this week?

....

....

....

I have the following things on this week: Academic exams, sport training, music lessons etc.

....

....

....

....

My Key Focus For This Week:

OCTOBER 2021

MONDAY 18

....
....
....
....

┌─ OTHER NOTES/TASKS TO COMPLETE ─────────────────────────────────┐
│   │
│   │
└──┘

TUESDAY 19

....
....
....
....

┌─ OTHER NOTES/TASKS TO COMPLETE ─────────────────────────────────┐
│   │
│   │
└──┘

WEDNESDAY 20

....
....
....
....

┌─ OTHER NOTES/TASKS TO COMPLETE ─────────────────────────────────┐
│   │
│   │
└──┘

THURSDAY 21

....
....
....
....

┌─ OTHER NOTES/TASKS TO COMPLETE ─────────────────────────────────┐
│   │
│   │
└──┘

FRIDAY 22

....
....
....
....

SAT 23	SUN 24

Homeroom Teacher _____   Parent Signature _____

My Week Ahead

Start your week by answering the following questions

I am grateful for:

....

....

What will be my act of kindness this week?

....

....

....

I have the following things on this week: Academic exams, sport training, music lessons etc.

....

....

....

....

My Key Focus For This Week:

OCTOBER 2021

MONDAY 25

....
....
....
....

┌─ OTHER NOTES/TASKS TO COMPLETE ──────────────────────────┐
│   │
│   │
└──┘

TUESDAY 26

....
....
....
....

┌─ OTHER NOTES/TASKS TO COMPLETE ──────────────────────────┐
│   │
│   │
└──┘

WEDNESDAY 27

....
....
....
....

┌─ OTHER NOTES/TASKS TO COMPLETE ──────────────────────────┐
│   │
│   │
└──┘

THURSDAY 28

....
....
....
....

┌─ OTHER NOTES/TASKS TO COMPLETE ──────────────────────────┐
│   │
│   │
└──┘

FRIDAY 29

....
....
....
....

SAT 30	SUN 31

Homeroom Teacher_____ **Parent Signature**_____

My Week Ahead

Start your week by answering the following questions

I am grateful for:

....

....

What will be my act of kindness this week?

....

....

....

I have the following things on this week: *Academic exams, sport training, music lessons etc.*

....

....

....

....

....

My Key Focus For This Week:

NOVEMBER 2021

MONDAY 01

....
....
....
....

┌─ OTHER NOTES/TASKS TO COMPLETE ──────────────────────────────────────┐
│   │
│   │
└──┘

TUESDAY 02

....
....
....
....

┌─ OTHER NOTES/TASKS TO COMPLETE ──────────────────────────────────────┐
│   │
│   │
└──┘

WEDNESDAY 03

....
....
....
....

┌─ OTHER NOTES/TASKS TO COMPLETE ──────────────────────────────────────┐
│   │
│   │
└──┘

THURSDAY 04

....
....
....
....

┌─ OTHER NOTES/TASKS TO COMPLETE ──────────────────────────────────────┐
│   │
│   │
└──┘

FRIDAY 05

....
....
....
....

SAT 06	**SUN 07**

Homeroom Teacher _____   Parent Signature _____

My Week Ahead

Start your week by answering the following questions

I am grateful for:

....

....

What will be my act of kindness this week?

....

....

I have the following things on this week: Academic exams, sport training, music lessons etc.

....

....

....

....

My Key Focus For This Week:

NOVEMBER 2021

MONDAY 08

....
....
....
....

┌─ OTHER NOTES/TASKS TO COMPLETE ────────────────────────────┐
│   │
│   │
└──┘

TUESDAY 09

....
....
....
....

┌─ OTHER NOTES/TASKS TO COMPLETE ────────────────────────────┐
│   │
│   │
└──┘

WEDNESDAY 10

....
....
....
....

┌─ OTHER NOTES/TASKS TO COMPLETE ────────────────────────────┐
│   │
│   │
└──┘

THURSDAY 11

....
....
....
....

┌─ OTHER NOTES/TASKS TO COMPLETE ────────────────────────────┐
│   │
│   │
└──┘

FRIDAY 12

....
....
....
....

SAT 13	SUN 14

Homeroom Teacher _____   **Parent Signature** _____

My Week Ahead

Start your week by answering the following questions

I am grateful for:

....

....

What will be my act of kindness this week?

....

....

....

I have the following things on this week: Academic exams, sport training, music lessons etc.

....

....

....

....

My Key Focus For This Week:

NOVEMBER 2021

MONDAY 15

....
....
....
....

┌─ OTHER NOTES/TASKS TO COMPLETE ──────────────────────────┐
│   │
│   │
└──┘

TUESDAY 16

....
....
....
....

┌─ OTHER NOTES/TASKS TO COMPLETE ──────────────────────────┐
│   │
│   │
└──┘

WEDNESDAY 17

....
....
....
....

┌─ OTHER NOTES/TASKS TO COMPLETE ──────────────────────────┐
│   │
│   │
└──┘

THURSDAY 18

....
....
....
....

┌─ OTHER NOTES/TASKS TO COMPLETE ──────────────────────────┐
│   │
│   │
└──┘

FRIDAY 19

....
....
....
....

SAT 20	SUN 21

Homeroom Teacher _____   **Parent Signature** _____

My Week Ahead

Start your week by answering the following questions

I am grateful for:

....

....

What will be my act of kindness this week?

....

....

....

I have the following things on this week: Academic exams, sport training, music lessons etc.

....

....

....

....

....

My Key Focus For This Week:

NOVEMBER 2021

MONDAY 22

....
....
....
....

┌─ OTHER NOTES/TASKS TO COMPLETE ───────────────────────────────┐
│   │
│   │
└──┘

TUESDAY 23

....
....
....
....

┌─ OTHER NOTES/TASKS TO COMPLETE ───────────────────────────────┐
│   │
│   │
└──┘

WEDNESDAY 24

....
....
....
....

┌─ OTHER NOTES/TASKS TO COMPLETE ───────────────────────────────┐
│   │
│   │
└──┘

THURSDAY 25

....
....
....
....

┌─ OTHER NOTES/TASKS TO COMPLETE ───────────────────────────────┐
│   │
│   │
└──┘

FRIDAY 26

....
....
....
....

SAT 27	**SUN 28**

Homeroom Teacher _____   **Parent Signature** _____

My Week Ahead

Start your week by answering the following questions

I am grateful for:
....
....

What will be my act of kindness this week?
....
....
....

I have the following things on this week: *Academic exams, sport training, music lessons etc.*
....
....
....
....
....

My Key Focus For This Week:

NOVEMBER/DECEMBER 2021

MONDAY 29

....
....
....
....

OTHER NOTES/TASKS TO COMPLETE

TUESDAY 30

....
....
....
....

OTHER NOTES/TASKS TO COMPLETE

WEDNESDAY 01

....
....
....
....

OTHER NOTES/TASKS TO COMPLETE

THURSDAY 02

....
....
....
....

OTHER NOTES/TASKS TO COMPLETE

FRIDAY 03

....
....
....
....

SAT 04	SUN 05

Homeroom Teacher _____ **Parent Signature** _____

My Week Ahead

Start your week by answering the following questions

I am grateful for:

....

....

What will be my act of kindness this week?

....

....

....

I have the following things on this week: Academic exams, sport training, music lessons etc.

....

....

....

....

....

My Key Focus For This Week:

DECEMBER 2021

MONDAY 13

....
....
....
....

OTHER NOTES/TASKS TO COMPLETE

TUESDAY 14

....
....
....
....

OTHER NOTES/TASKS TO COMPLETE

WEDNESDAY 15

....
....
....
....

OTHER NOTES/TASKS TO COMPLETE

THURSDAY 16

....
....
....
....

OTHER NOTES/TASKS TO COMPLETE

FRIDAY 17

....
....
....
....

SAT 18	SUN 19

Homeroom Teacher_____ Parent Signature_____

Notes, Messages and Signatures From Friends, Family and Teachers

My Week Ahead

Start your week by answering the following questions

I am grateful for:

....

....

What will be my act of kindness this week?

....

....

....

I have the following things on this week: Academic exams, sport training, music lessons etc.

....

....

....

....

....

My Key Focus For This Week:

DECEMBER 2021

MONDAY 06

....
....
....
....

┌─ OTHER NOTES/TASKS TO COMPLETE ───┐
│   │
│   │
└───┘

TUESDAY 07

....
....
....
....

┌─ OTHER NOTES/TASKS TO COMPLETE ───┐
│   │
│   │
└───┘

WEDNESDAY 08

....
....
....
....

┌─ OTHER NOTES/TASKS TO COMPLETE ───┐
│   │
│   │
└───┘

THURSDAY 09

....
....
....
....

┌─ OTHER NOTES/TASKS TO COMPLETE ───┐
│   │
│   │
└───┘

FRIDAY 10

....
....
....
....

SAT 11	SUN 12

Homeroom Teacher _____   **Parent Signature** _____

School Term Notes

www.ingramcontent.com/pod-product-compliance
Lightning Source LLC
LaVergne TN
LVHW060141080526
838202LV00049B/4046